Sensei Self Development

Mental Health Chronicles Series

Finding Ways to Connect with Others

Sensei Paul David

Copyright Page

Sensei Self Development -
Finding Ways to Connect with Others,
by Sensei Paul David

Copyright © 2024

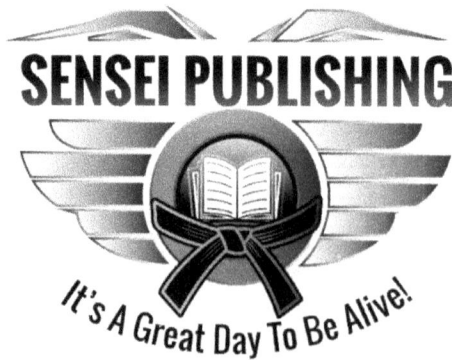

SENSEI PUBLISHING

It's A Great Day To Be Alive!

www.senseipublishing.com

@senseipublishing
#senseipublishing

Get/Share Your FREE SSD Mental Health Chronicles at
www.senseiselfdevelopment.care

or

CLICK HERE

Sensei Self Development

FOR ADULTS

An Introduction to Mindfulness

Sensei Paul David

Check Out The SSD Chronicles Series CLICK HERE

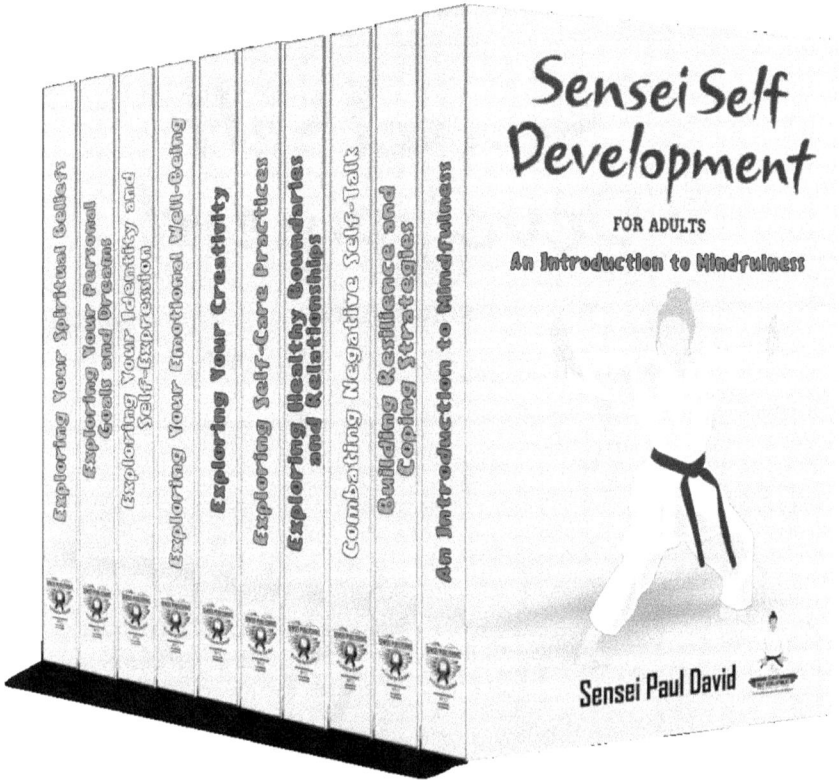

Exploring Your Spiritual Beliefs

Exploring Your Personal Goals and Dreams

Exploring Your Identity and Self-Expression

Exploring Your Emotional Well-Being

Exploring Your Creativity

Exploring Self-Care Practices

Exploring Healthy Boundaries and Relationships

Combating Negative Self-Talk

Building Resilience and Coping Strategies

An Introduction to Mindfulness

Sensei Self Development

FOR ADULTS

An Introduction to Mindfulness

Sensei Paul David

Dedication

To those who courageously take action towards self-improvement - you are helping to evolve the world for generations to come.

- It's a great day to be alive!

If Found Please Contact:

_____

Reward If Found:

_____

MY
COMMITMENT

I, _____
commit to writing This Sensei Self
Development Journal for at least 10 days in a
row, starting: _____

Writing this journal is valuable to me because:

_____

_____

_____

_____

_____

_____

If I finish a minimum of 10 consecutive days of
writing in this journal, I will reward myself by:

_____

_____

_____

_____

_____

_____

If I don't finish 10 days of writing this journal, I will promise to:

_____

_____

_____

_____

_____

I will do the following things to ensure that I write in my Sensei Self Development Journal every day:

_____

_____

_____

_____

_____

Get/Share Your FREE All-Ages Mental Health eBook Now at

www.senseiselfdevelopment.com

Or CLICK HERE

senseiselfdevelopment.com

Check Out Another Book In The
SSD BOOK SERIES:

senseipublishing.com/SSD_SERIES

CLICK HERE

SENSEI SELF DEVELOPMENT
BOOKS SERIES

senseiselfdevelopment.senseipublishing.com

Join Our Publishing Journey!

If you would like to receive FUTURE FREE BOOKS and get to know us better, please click www.senseipublishing.com and join our newsletter by entering your email address in the pop-up box.

Follow Our Blog: senseipauldavid.ca

Follow/Like/Subscribe: Facebook, Instagram, YouTube: @senseipublishing

Scan the QR Code with your phone or tablet

to follow us on social media: Like / Subscribe / Follow

A Message From The Author:
Sensei Paul David

Dear Reader,

Welcome to the world of mental health journaling – a sacred space for self-reflection, growth, and healing. Within these pages, you hold the power to uplift your spirit, invigorate your mind, and nourish your goals.

In a world that often moves at blink-and-you'll-miss-it speed, it's crucial to make time for self-care and self-discovery.

Anxiety, stress, and emotional turbulence may have clouded your mind, making it difficult to find clarity and peace within. But fear not! Together, we will navigate the labyrinth of emotions, and experiences, helping to simplify the path to mental well-being.

This journal is not merely a bunch of blank pages awaiting your words. It is your compassionate companion, offering solace and understanding during your unique journey. Here, you are free to unburden yourself, celebrate small and large victories, and confront the challenges that may still linger.

Within the sheltered realm of these pages, there is no judgment, no expectation, and no pressure. Your unique experience and perspective hold immeasurable worth, and your voice deserves to be heard. Whether you choose to fill the lines with eloquence or simply scribble fragments of your thoughts, please remember each entry is a valuable contribution to your growth.

In this sacred space, you are challenged to take off the mask we so often wear in the outside world. It is here that you can be raw, vulnerable, and authentic – allowing your true self to be seen and embraced without reservation. By giving yourself permission to explore the depths of your emotions and confront the shadows that may lurk within, you will discover profound insights and find the healing you seek over time.

As you embark on this journaling journey, I encourage you to embrace the process itself rather than fixate solely on the outcome. Remember, it is not about reaching a certain destination or ticking off boxes on a list of accomplishments. Rather, it is about cultivating self-awareness, fostering self-compassion, and nurturing a sense of curiosity about the intricate workings of your intelligently beautiful mind.

In the quiet moments of reflection, let your pen become a bridge between your inner world and the possibilities that lie ahead. Create a sanctuary for your thoughts, fears, triumphs, and dreams. As you pour your heart onto these pages, allow your words to be a living testament to courage, resilience, and an unwavering commitment to your own well-being.

I am honored to be a part of your journey, and I believe in your ability to navigate the twists and turns with grace and resilience. Remember, you are not alone in this – countless others have walked similar paths, faced similar challenges, and emerged stronger and wiser on the other side. You have the power to reclaim all of your untapped joy, cultivate a positive mindset that serves you, and foster a deep sense of self-love and peaceful confident. – And it will take a worth effort and time.

So, open the first page of this journal with hope, curiosity, and an open heart and open mind. Embrace the transformative power of self-reflection, and allow it to guide you towards a life of greater fulfilment and peace. Each journaling session is an opportunity to not only connect with yourself but also to rekindle the light within that sometimes flickers but never extinguishes.

Remember, the pages you are about to fill are not just a record of your journey but also a testament to your strength, resilience, and indomitable spirit. Cherish this space, invest in yourself, and let your words be an ode to the magnificent journey of becoming whole.

With great respect for your decision to evolve,

Paul

MY CONVICTION

Please circle your answers below

I am DECIDING to be patient with myself and this PROCESS each time I journal toward my improved state of mental well-being

YES   NO

"The present moment is filled with joy and happiness. If you are attentive, you will see it."

Thich Nhat Hanh

Introduction

In a world increasingly defined by digital screens and virtual interactions, the art of connecting with others face-to-face has never been more crucial. The essence of human connection lies in our ability to understand, empathize, and engage with each other in meaningful ways. This connection is not just a social nicety; it's a fundamental need, deeply rooted in our psychology and evolution.

Humans are social creatures by nature. From the dawn of civilization, our survival has hinged on our ability to work together, communicate effectively, and build relationships. These skills have shaped our history, from forming tribes for hunting and gathering to building vast empires and advanced societies. As we navigate the complexities of the modern world, the need for genuine connections remains as important as ever.

However, in today's fast-paced and technology-driven world, we often find ourselves isolated, despite being more 'connected' than ever before. Social media, while valuable for keeping in touch across distances, can sometimes replace deeper, more meaningful interactions with a stream of updates and surface-level engagement.

The art of conversation, the joy of shared experiences, and the growth that comes from real human interaction are at risk of being lost in the digital shuffle.

Yet, the hunger for real connection persists. It's evident in the way we cherish moments spent with loved ones, the fulfillment we find in helping others, and the sense of community we feel when we come together for a common cause. It's in these moments that we find our shared humanity, our capacity for kindness, and our innate ability to understand and support one another.

The journey towards better connecting with others starts with recognizing this innate need and valuing the richness it brings to our lives. It involves honing our listening skills, being present in our interactions, and showing empathy towards others' experiences and perspectives. It's about finding common ground amidst our differences and building bridges where there are gaps in understanding.

Importance of Connecting With Others

Understanding the deep-rooted need for human connection, it's clear that our interactions with others are more than just social niceties; they are essential to our well-being. When we engage with people, whether they're close family members, friends, or even acquaintances, it impacts our mental and physical health in profound ways.

The warmth of a genuine connection can light up neural pathways in our brain, releasing endorphins and other positive chemicals like oxytocin. These chemicals help reduce stress and anxiety, fostering a sense of calm and well-being. It's akin to the feeling of warmth and safety, like being wrapped in a soft blanket on a cold day.

Moreover, these interactions shape our perception and understanding of the world.

Engaging in diverse conversations exposes us to new ideas and perspectives, fostering empathy and a deeper understanding of the human experience. It's like opening a window to different worlds, where we learn not just about others, but also about ourselves.

In terms of physical health, the benefits are just as striking. Studies have shown that individuals with strong social networks tend to have stronger immune systems, lower blood pressure, and even a longer lifespan. It's as if our bodies are designed to thrive on social interaction, with isolation being detrimental to our health.

In the workplace, the power of connection translates into more effective teamwork, innovation, and job satisfaction. When people feel connected to their colleagues, they're more likely to collaborate effectively and support each other, leading to a more positive and productive work environment.

So, connecting with others is a fundamental part of being human that nourishes our mental, emotional, and physical health. It's the invisible thread that ties us to the rest of humanity.

But what happens when we don't connect with others i.e. when you are lonely?

Loneliness can lead to significant health issues such as disrupted sleep patterns, elevated blood pressure, and increased levels of cortisol, a stress hormone. It can weaken the immune system and diminish overall contentment. Loneliness is also a risk factor for antisocial behavior, depression, and even suicide.

Older individuals are particularly susceptible to loneliness, especially when decreased mobility makes socializing challenging. Yet, those who stay connected with others and maintain strong relationships tend to have a better quality of life, feel more satisfied, have a lower risk of dementia and mental decline, and need less domestic support.

Younger people, including teenagers and those in their 20s, are also at risk when isolated. Lack of social relationships can directly impact their physical health, increasing the risk of obesity, inflammation, and high blood pressure, which can lead to long-term health problems like heart disease, stroke, and cancer. However, a diverse social network can help mitigate these risks.

It's important to recognize that loneliness differs from solitude. While loneliness is a problem, solitude may not be. Many people live alone and lead happy, fulfilling lives. But they too connect with others.

Fast Facts

1. Friendship Development: A study by Jeffrey A. Hall found that it takes about 50 hours of time together to move from acquaintance to casual friend, 90 hours to go from that to simple 'friend,' and more than 200 hours before you can consider someone your close friend.

2. Watching vs. Socializing in America: Research indicates that on average, Americans spend about 2.5 hours a day watching movies or TV shows but only about 30 minutes socializing and communicating with others.

3. Long-Term Impact of Friendships: Studies suggest that the quantity and quality of friendships in early adulthood can have long-lasting effects on wellbeing up to 30 years later, influencing happiness and overall life satisfaction.

4. Impact of Social Media on Relationships: Research published in the American Journal of Preventive Medicine found that heavy use of social media is associated with feelings of social isolation. Contrarily, moderate use can enhance existing relationships.

5. Power of Active Listening: A study in the Journal of Research in Personality showed that active listeners are perceived as more socially attractive and desirable as friends. Active listening contributes significantly to relationship building.

6. Laughter and Bonding: A study from the University of North Carolina found that couples

who laugh together report having higher-quality relationships. Laughter triggers endorphin release, which promotes social bonding.

7. Gratitude in Relationships: Research in the Journal of Personality and Social Psychology indicates that expressing gratitude to a partner can improve the quality of the relationship and increase the connection between partners.

8. Shared Experiences and Friendship: Findings suggest that shared experiences, especially challenging or novel ones, can accelerate friendship development. This is linked to the concept of "misattribution of arousal," where an exciting situation can enhance interpersonal attraction.

9. Influence of Physical Touch: Studies have shown that simple physical contact, like hugs or handshakes, can build trust and cooperation, indicating the powerful role of non-verbal communication in human relationships.

How to Connect With Others

Self-Disclosure

Self-disclosure is like opening a window into your world for someone else to peek through. It's about sharing those bits and pieces of your life – your thoughts, feelings, experiences – with someone else. When you share something personal, it's like you're saying, "I trust you with this piece of me."

However, it's important to share at a pace that feels right – not too little, not too much. It's about finding that sweet spot where both people feel comfortable and heard.

Remember, everyone's comfort level with sharing is different, and that's okay. It's like each person has their own unique recipe for self-disclosure. What matters is that there's an exchange – a bit of give and take.

An insightful study in self-disclosure was conducted by psychologists Dr. Erin E. Bonar and Dr. Carl W. Lejuez. In this study, groups of adolescents who were not previously acquainted were asked to participate in structured interactions. These interactions included activities designed to encourage varying levels of self-disclosure, from discussing favorite movies or music to sharing personal experiences and challenges.

The findings indicated that higher levels of self-disclosure were strongly correlated with the development of closer, more meaningful friendships among the participants. Adolescents who shared more personal information were more likely to report feelings of closeness and trust with their peers.

In another study done similarly, but to gauge happiness, the participants reported increased levels of wellbeing and happiness after having intimate conversation with a stranger.

So self-disclosure not only helps you in connecting with others, but also makes you feel happier. And we will see this again and again – the link between stronger connection and happiness. This should not be surprising to you since relationship satisfaction is the most significant factor that determines an individual's happiness. More than wealth. More than status.

Reciprocity

Reciprocity is like the idea of "you scratch my back, and I'll scratch yours." It means when someone does something nice for you, you feel a natural urge to do something nice in return and vice versa.

Imagine you're sharing a meal with a friend. You offer them the last piece of your favorite dish, not expecting anything in return. A week later, they surprise you with a small gift, a token of appreciation. This is reciprocity in action – a natural, heartfelt exchange that deepens bonds and fosters trust.

But reciprocity goes beyond just physical exchanges. It's also about emotional and social give and take. When someone shares their time, listens to your stories, or offers support during tough times, they're engaging in an emotional form of reciprocity. By responding in kind, you create a cycle of support and understanding.

By doing favors or being kind to others, you can create a positive cycle where people feel inclined to help you in return. This strengthens friendships, family bonds, and professional relationships.

So if you want to get closer to someone, lend an ear, help them out, or buy them a coffee.

Sharing Positive Vibes

Research demonstrates that people form connections by sharing positive emotions. This connection isn't just psychological; when two individuals experience good vibes, their bodies synchronize. They mimic each other's gestures, facial expressions, and even have similar changes in heart rate and hormones.

From infancy, humans rely on these positive, synchronized moments as a fundamental way to connect, and they continue seeking such interactions throughout life. Think of enjoyable activities like singing and dancing together – they foster a real sense of connection and release endorphins. The same applies to shared laughter, which not only strengthens bonds but also indicates a shared sense of reality, deepening the connection.

When someone shares a positive event in their life, a reliable way to strengthen your bond is to genuinely and enthusiastically respond with celebration, congratulations, and a heartfelt "I'm so happy for you."

Researchers at the University of California, Berkeley, discovered that when people in relationships say things like "I love you" and show appreciation often, it makes their relationships happier and more stable.

Another study found that when people hug, hold hands, or show physical affection, it makes a special hormone called oxytocin, which helps build trust and connections between them.

Celebrating Good Fortune

When we share good news from our lives and receive positive responses, it's known as capitalization in psychology. This can be as simple as a high-five, a heartfelt "congratulations," or an enthusiastic "I'm so glad to hear that!" Studies have revealed that in relationships, capitalization plays a crucial role in building trust. It demonstrates our genuine care and interest in each other's lives, strengthening the bond between us.

Sharing Laughter

Research has demonstrated that sharing laughter can create a genuine sense of connection. The important factor here is that we engage in friendly and affiliative humor, where our jokes are meant to be light-hearted and not hurtful. It's crucial to distinguish this from humor that may involve putting others down. When everyone involved genuinely finds amusement in the humor or silliness, it fosters a feeling of connection and camaraderie.

Moving in Sync

Numerous studies have explored the concept of synchronizing physical movements and its impact on human bonding. For example, research involving group dancing and singing has consistently shown that when individuals engage in coordinated physical activities, they tend to feel a greater sense of closeness and connection with one another. This phenomenon can be attributed to the release of hormones associated with social bonding during these activities.

Furthermore, studies conducted with students instructed to walk in lock-step or perform synchronized exercises have yielded similar results. In these cases, individuals reported feeling a heightened sense of unity and connection with their peers. This suggests that engaging in activities that involve physical synchronization can be an effective and tangible way to foster a sense of togetherness and strengthen social bonds.

Complementing

I use this heavily, but you have to be careful that you don't lie. Compliment things that you genuinely find good in the other person and tell them that. And be specific. If you are not specific, it can sound as if you are lying. If you speak the truth, most likely the person has already noticed it in themselves. They might know that it's a good feature that they have or they might be unsure. Either way, you will induce positive emotions in them when you point it out.

Two things you should know about complimenting:

- Compliments not only make the receiver feel good but also improve the mood of the giver.

- Research shows that compliments have a greater positive impact on the receiver than most people anticipate.

In a study published in the Personality and Social Psychology Bulletin, Vanessa Bohns, explored how people feel before and after giving or receiving compliments.

They started with an experiment on a college campus. Participants were asked to compliment the fourth person of the same gender they met. Before they began, they shared their thoughts about giving compliments. Their task was simple: give a nice comment about the person's clothing, like "I like your shirt," and then hand them a survey in a sealed envelope.

What they found was quite interesting. The people giving compliments didn't realize just how happy their words would make others feel. The recipients of the compliments ended up feeling much happier and more flattered than the givers expected.

In a second experiment, participants were free to compliment anything they genuinely liked about others. Again, the givers underestimated how much their kind words would mean. Even after seeing the positive reactions, they still didn't realize the full impact of their compliments.

In a third study, the researchers addressed the question: do people avoid giving compliments to strangers because they worry about making them feel awkward or uncomfortable? This time, they asked the compliment-givers to predict whether the recipients would have negative feelings about receiving a compliment. The results showed that the givers "drastically overestimated how bothered, uncomfortable, and annoyed" the receiver would feel. This likely deters people from giving more compliments.

So don't worry, give compliments generously.

Gossiping

Gossip is something we all engage in, no matter what that old saying tells, "If you have nothing nice to say, don't say anything at all." Whether we're catching up at the office, sharing family updates, or firing off texts in our group chats, talking about others is just part of the human experience. A study in 1993 found that both males (55%) and females (67%) dedicated a good chunk of their conversations to this stuff.

Now, when we think about gossip, it often conjures images of mean-spirited rumors or celebrity drama. But here's the thing – researchers see it in a broader light. Psychologists describe it as "talking about people who aren't around." It's basically a natural part of our social fabric – a way we connect, share information, and build our communities.

Gossip isn't always a bad thing. It can actually be quite positive or just plain neutral. In a study from 2019, they found that out of the 52 minutes people spent gossiping daily, about three-quarters of it was just everyday conversation, nothing scandalous. Negative gossip made up only a small slice, around 15%, and positive gossip was even less common, at just 9%. So, while we do chat about others quite a bit, most of it is just harmless chit-chat.

Communication for Better Relationship

1. Avoid Conversational Narcissism: Don't steer every conversation back to yourself. Show genuine interest in what others have to say, rather than using their comments as a springboard to talk about your own experiences.

Example: Your friend mentions they're having trouble at work. Instead of saying, "I had the same issue at my job," ask them, "What's been happening at work that's troubling you?"

2. Don't Interrupt: Allow others to finish their thoughts without interjecting. Interrupting can signal impatience or lack of respect for the speaker's viewpoint.

Example: If someone is explaining their weekend plans and you're eager to share yours, resist the urge to cut in. Wait until they finish, then share your plans.

3. Stay Away from Constant Advice-Giving: While it's natural to want to help, not everyone is looking for advice. Sometimes, people just need a listening ear. Offer advice only when it's asked for.

Example: If a colleague is venting about a difficult project, instead of immediately offering solutions, you could repeat their words back and agree with them.

4. Avoid One-Upping: When someone shares an experience, resist the urge to top it with a story of your own. This can make the other person feel like their experience is being minimized.

Example: If a friend tells you they ran 5 miles, resist the urge to respond with, "That's great! I ran 10 miles yesterday!" Instead, you might say, "That's awesome! How did you feel after your run?"

5. Don't Dominate the Conversation: Ensure that the conversation is a balanced exchange. If you find you've been speaking for a while, invite the other person to share their thoughts.

Example: After sharing a detailed story about your weekend, ask the other person, "How was your weekend?"

6. Steer Clear of Constantly Changing the Subject: Respect the natural flow of the conversation. Constantly changing the topic

can make it seem like you're not interested in what the other person has to say.

Example: If your friend is talking about a movie they recently saw, don't abruptly switch to talking about your new diet. Show interest in their topic before moving on to yours.

7. Be Wary of Being Judgmental: Keep an open mind and avoid passing judgment on others' opinions and experiences.

Example: If someone shares a political opinion different from yours, instead of saying, "I can't believe you think that," try, "That's an interesting perspective. Can you tell me more about why you feel that way?"

8. Avoid Excessive Negative Talk: While it's fine to share concerns or frustrations, dwelling too much on negative topics can be draining for others.

Example: If you've been complaining about your job for several minutes, shift the conversation by saying, "But enough about my job woes. I'd love to hear about your new hobby!"

9. Don't Make Assumptions: Don't assume you know what the other person is thinking or feeling. If in doubt, ask them.

Example: Instead of assuming a friend is upset because they're quiet, ask them, "You seem a bit quiet today. Is everything okay?"

10. Avoid Multitasking During Conversations: Give your full attention to the conversation. Avoid looking at your phone or doing other tasks while someone is speaking to you.

Example: If you're chatting with someone and receive a text message, resist the urge to look at your phone. Instead, maintain eye contact and focus on the conversation.

By being mindful of these aspects, you can create a more positive, engaging, and respectful conversational environment. Remember, effective communication is about making the other person feel heard, respected, and valued.

Focus on Quality Over Quantity

One sociological study pointed out that in 1985, Americans, on average, had three close friends, but by 2004, the most common number was zero, with over a quarter of Americans reporting they had no one to confide in. This decline in social connectedness may account for the rising levels of loneliness, isolation, and the increasing demand for psychological counseling.

The good news is that social connection is more about your subjective feeling of connection than the number of friends you have. Even with a large number of friends, you might feel lonely, whereas having no close friends or relatives doesn't necessarily mean you can't feel connected.

This shows the importance of nurturing quality relationships and the subjective experience of connection for both mental and physical health.

Developing meaningful connections, focusing on quality interactions, and cultivating a sense of belonging are crucial for overall well-being

Have you heard of the expression "being lonely in the crowd"? That's not good. So pick and choose your relationship.

- Remove people that are toxic, negative, or drain on your energy levels.
- Add people that give you energy or make you feel good after you hang out with them.
- Stay away from people who consistently leave you feeling bad about yourself

Before We Get Started…

Remember, mindfulness journaling is a personal practice, and these questions are meant to guide and inspire you. Feel free to adapt and modify them to suit your needs and preferences. Explore, reflect, and embrace the opportunity to deepen your self-awareness and cultivate a sense of inner peace.

Date ___ / ___ / ___ : S   M   T   W   Th   F   S

I feel:
(please circle)

because   because   because   because   because

_____ _____ _____ _____ _____

_____ _____ _____ _____ _____

Today I Am Grateful For

1. _____

2. _____

3. _____

What could help transform today into a remarkable day?

Reflective Writing

How have I helped others find ways to connect with me?

_____

_____

_____

_____

_____

_____

_____

What is the most effective way to introduce yourself to someone new?

A) By smiling and making eye contact
B) By using a firm handshake
C) By asking them personal questions
D) By sending them a friend request on social media

All Are Correct - Choose The Response You Feel Is Most Important To Remember

Date ___ / ___ / ___: S   M   T   W   Th   F   S

I feel:
(please circle)

because   because   because   because   because
_____   _____   _____   _____   _____
_____   _____   _____   _____   _____

Today I Am Grateful For

1. _____
2. _____
3. _____

What could help transform today into a remarkable day?

Reflective Writing

What are some of my successes in finding ways to connect with others?

_____

_____

_____

_____

_____

_____

_____

What is a great way to initiate a conversation with a stranger?

A) By complimenting their outfit or accessories
B) By sharing a personal story
C) By discussing a current event
D) By talking about your favorite TV show

All Are Correct - Choose The Response You Feel Is Most Important To Remember

Date ___ / ___ / ___ : S M T W Th F S

I feel:
(please circle)

because   because   because   because   because

_____ _____ _____ _____ _____

_____ _____ _____ _____ _____

Today I Am Grateful For

1. _____
2. _____
3. _____

What could help transform today into a remarkable day?

Reflective Writing

What have I learned about myself and others in the process
of finding and sustaining meaningful connections?

_____

_____

_____

_____

_____

_____

_____

What is the best way to maintain a long distance friendship?

A) By sending frequent text messages
B) By Skype or video calling regularly
C) By planning occasional visits
D) By constantly following each other's social media accounts

All Are Correct - Choose The Response You Feel Is Most Important To Remember

Date ___ / ___ / ___ : S M T W Th F S

I feel:
(please circle)

because _____ because _____ because _____ because _____ because _____

Today I Am Grateful For

1. _____
2. _____
3. _____

What could help transform today into a remarkable day?

Reflective Writing

What strategies have I used to make and maintain connections with others?

_____

_____

_____

_____

_____

_____

_____

How can you make someone feel valued during a conversation?

A) By actively listening and maintaining eye contact

B) By interrupting them to share your own opinions

C) By constantly checking your phone for notifications

D) By dominating the conversation with your own stories

All Are Correct - Choose The Response You Feel Is Most Important To Remember

Date ___ / ___ / ___ : S M T W Th F S

I feel:
(please circle)

because because because because because

_____ _____ _____ _____ _____

_____ _____ _____ _____ _____

Today I Am Grateful For

1. _____
2. _____
3. _____

What could help transform today into a remarkable day?

Reflective Writing

What are some of the obstacles I have faced in the journey of connecting with others?

_____

_____

_____

_____

_____

_____

_____

What is an effective way to show empathy towards someone?

A) By saying "I understand" and offering advice

B) By avoiding the topic or changing the subject

C) By listening without judgment and offering support

D) By criticizing or blaming them for their situation

All Are Correct - Choose The Response You Feel Is Most Important To Remember

Date ___ / ___ / ___: S M T W Th F S

I feel:
(please circle)

because _____   because _____   because _____   because _____   because _____

Today I Am Grateful For

1. _____
2. _____
3. _____

What could help transform today into a remarkable day?

Reflective Writing

In what ways have I been able to empathize and understand the perspectives of those I am trying to connect with

_____

_____

_____

_____

_____

_____

_____

What is a great way to connect with coworkers?

A) By sharing personal details and forming close friendships
B) By only talking about work-related topics
C) By gossiping about other coworkers
D) By avoiding social interactions with coworkers

All Are Correct - Choose The Response You Feel Is Most Important To Remember

Date ___ / ___ / ___: S M T W Th F S

I feel:
(please circle)

because because because because because

_____ _____ _____ _____ _____

_____ _____ _____ _____ _____

Today I Am Grateful For

1. _____

2. _____

3. _____

What could help transform today into a remarkable day?

Reflective Writing

What have I learned about the importance of listening and understanding in order to build connections?

_____

_____

_____

_____

_____

_____

_____

_____

What is an effective way to make new friends in a new city?

A) By joining clubs or groups that align with your interests
B) By staying at home and avoiding social events
C) By only reaching out to people you already know
D) By constantly comparing your new city to your old one

All Are Correct - Choose The Response You Feel Is Most Important To Remember

Date ___ / ___ / ___ : S   M   T   W   Th   F   S

I feel:
(please circle)

because   because   because   because   because
_____   _____   _____   _____   _____
_____   _____   _____   _____   _____

Today I Am Grateful For

1. _____
2. _____
3. _____

What could help transform today into a remarkable day?

Reflective Writing

What have I found to be the most rewarding
aspects of connecting with people?

_____

_____

_____

_____

_____

_____

_____

What is the most appropriate way to handle conflicts in a relationship?

A) By communicating openly and honestly

B) By ignoring the issue and hoping it will go away

C) By talking badly about the other person behind their back

D) By blaming the other person and refusing to take responsibility

All Are Correct - Choose The Response You Feel Is Most Important To Remember

Date ___ / ___ / ___: S   M   T   W   Th   F   S

I feel: (please circle)

because _____ because _____ because _____ because _____ because _____

Today I Am Grateful For

1. _____
2. _____
3. _____

What could help transform today into a remarkable day?

Reflective Writing

How has connecting with others helped me to grow and develop as a person?

_____

_____

_____

_____

_____

_____

_____

_____

What is a great way to show interest in someone during a conversation?

A) By constantly checking your phone for notifications
B) By asking them personal questions and actively listening
C) By interrupting them to change the topic
D) By talking about yourself and your accomplishments

All Are Correct - Choose The Response You Feel Is Most Important To Remember

Date ___ / ___ / ___ : S   M   T   W   Th   F   S

I feel:
(please circle)

because   because   because   because   because

_____   _____   _____   _____   _____

_____   _____   _____   _____   _____

Today I Am Grateful For

1. _____
2. _____
3. _____

What could help transform today into a remarkable day?

Reflective Writing

What have been my biggest challenges when it comes to connecting with others

_____

_____

_____

_____

_____

_____

_____

How can you make a positive first impression on someone?

A) By being genuine and authentic
B) By pretending to be someone you're not
C) By boasting about your achievements
D) By arriving late and making excuses

All Are Correct - Choose The Response You Feel Is Most Important To Remember

Date ___ / ___ / ___ : S   M   T   W   Th   F   S

I feel:
(please circle)

because because because because because
_____ _____ _____ _____ _____
_____ _____ _____ _____ _____

Today I Am Grateful For

1. _____
2. _____
3. _____

What could help transform today into a remarkable day?

Reflective Writing

How have I grown and changed as a result of connecting with people?

_____

_____

_____

_____

_____

_____

_____

What is an effective way to build trust in a relationship?

A) By constantly lying and manipulating the other person
B) By being unreliable and flaky
C) By being consistent and keeping your promises
D) By avoiding difficult conversations and conflicts

All Are Correct - Choose The Response You Feel Is Most Important To Remember

Date ___ / ___ / ___ : S   M   T   W   Th   F   S

I feel:
(please circle)

because _____ because _____ because _____ because _____ because _____

Today I Am Grateful For

1. _____
2. _____
3. _____

What could help transform today into a remarkable day?

Reflective Writing
What have been some of the most meaningful connections I have made?

_____

_____

_____

_____

_____

_____

_____

_____

How can you overcome shyness and connect with others?

A) By avoiding social interactions and isolating yourself

B) By practicing assertiveness and speaking up for yourself

C) By pretending to be outgoing and overly friendly

D) By relying on alcohol or drugs to loosen up

All Are Correct - Choose The Response You Feel Is Most Important To Remember

Date ___ / ___ / ___: S M T W Th F S

I feel:
(please circle)

☺ because _____
😁 because _____
😋 because _____
😣 because _____
😠 because _____

Today I Am Grateful For

1. _____
2. _____
3. _____

What could help transform today into a remarkable day?

Reflective Writing
How have I been able to embrace diversity when connecting with others?

_____

_____

_____

_____

_____

_____

_____

_____

What is an appropriate boundary to set in a friendship?

A) By sharing intimate details of your personal life

B) By respecting each other's privacy and boundaries

C) By constantly seeking approval and validation from each other

D) By constantly competing and comparing each other's achievements

All Are Correct - Choose The Response You Feel Is Most Important To Remember

Date ___ / ___ / ___ : S M T W Th F S

I feel:
(please circle)

because   because   because   because   because
_____   _____   _____   _____   _____
_____   _____   _____   _____   _____

Today I Am Grateful For

1. _____
2. _____
3. _____

What could help transform today into a remarkable day?

Reflective Writing

What have been my best practices when it comes
to finding ways to connect with others?

_____

_____

_____

_____

_____

_____

_____

What is an effective way to handle a disagreement with someone?

A) By yelling and getting angry

B) By avoiding the issue and pretending everything is okay

C) By listening to the other person's perspective and finding a compromise

D) By talking badly about the other person behind their back

All Are Correct - Choose The Response You Feel Is Most Important To Remember

Date ___ / ___ / ___ : S   M   T   W   Th   F   S

I feel: (please circle)

because _____ because _____ because _____ because _____ because _____

Today I Am Grateful For

1. _____
2. _____
3. _____

What could help transform today into a remarkable day?

Reflective Writing

What advice would I give to others who are trying to find ways to connect with people?

_____

_____

_____

_____

_____

_____

_____

How can you make a positive impact in your community?

A) By getting involved in community service projects
B) By complaining and criticizing everything
C) By avoiding social events and interactions
D) By only focusing on your own personal success

All Are Correct - Choose The Response You Feel Is Most Important To Remember

As we reach the final pages of this journey through "Positive Mindset," I want to extend my heartfelt thanks to you. Your commitment to exploring positivity and its transformative power is not only commendable but a testament to your desire for personal growth and a richer, more fulfilling life experience.

Remember, the journey towards a positive mindset is ongoing and ever-evolving. Each day presents new opportunities to apply these principles, to learn, and to grow. I encourage you to revisit these pages whenever you need a reminder of your incredible potential to foster positivity and resilience in the face of life's challenges.

As we part ways, I leave you with a quote that has been a guiding star in my journey: "The greatest discovery of any generation is that a human can alter his life by altering his attitude."

— William James.

Thank you for allowing me to be a part of your journey. May your path be filled with light, hope, and endless possibilities. Farewell, and may you carry the spirit of positivity with you, today and always.

With gratitude and best wishes,

Sensei Paul David

Reflective Writing

_____

_____

_____

_____

_____

_____

_____

_____

_____

_____

_____

_____

_____

_____

_____

_____

_____

_____

_____

_____

_____

_____

_____

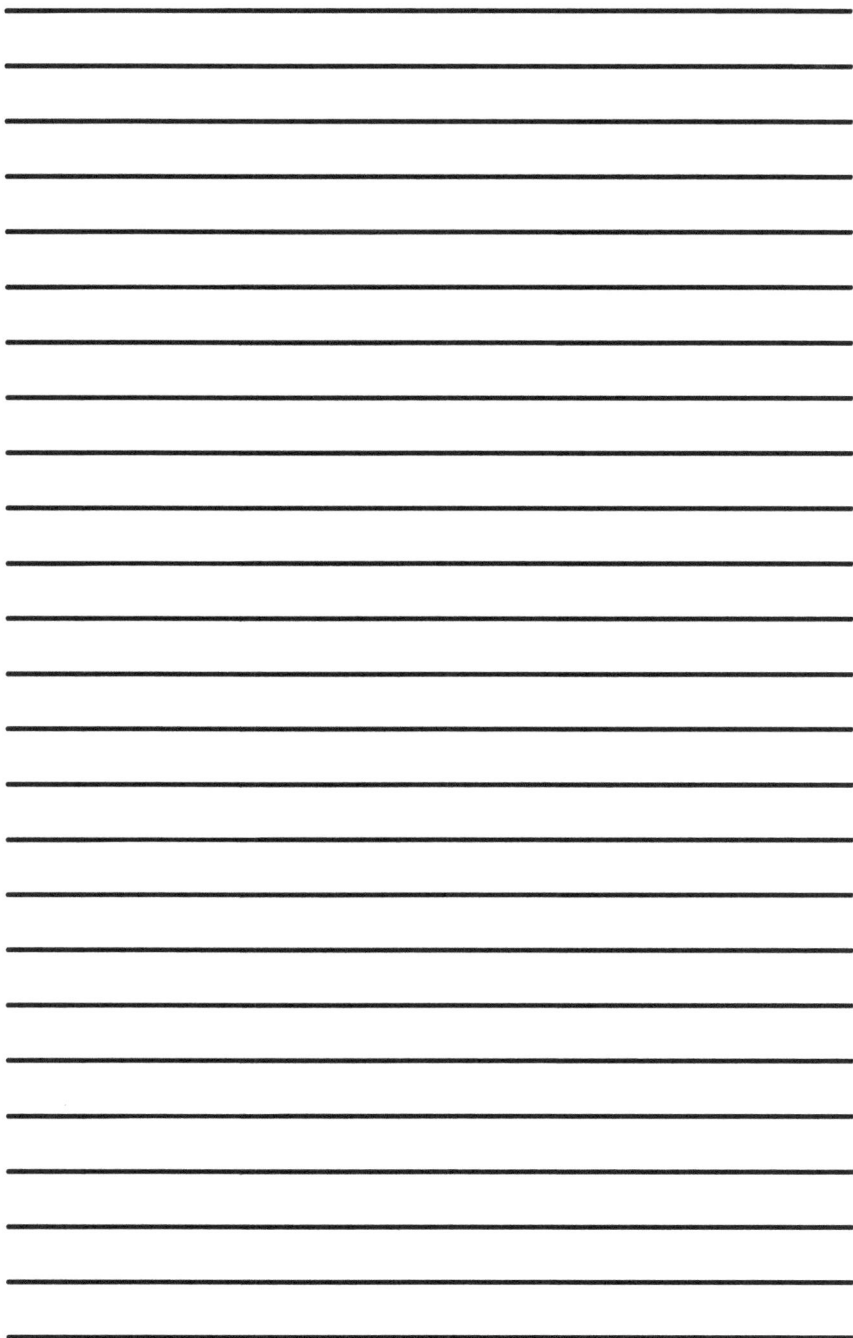

The End

As you close the pages of this mindfulness journal, remember that each word you've written is a step on your journey towards self-awareness and inner peace. Embrace the moments of clarity, the revelations, and even the uncertainties you've encountered along the way. Let this journal be a testament to your growth and a reminder that every day offers a new opportunity to be present, to observe, and to appreciate the simple wonders of life. Carry these lessons forward, and may your path be filled with mindful moments and serene reflections. Until we meet again in these pages, be gentle with yourself and stay anchored in the now.

Mindfulness isn't difficult, we just need to remember to do it.

Thank You!

If you found this book helpful, I would be grateful if you would **post an honest review on Amazon** so this book can reach other supportive readers like you!

All you need to do is digitally flip to the back and leave your review. Or visit amazon.com/author/senseipauldavid click the correct book cover and click on the blue link next to the yellow stars that say, "customer reviews."

As always...
It's a great day to be alive!

Get/Share Your FREE SSD Mental Health Chronicles at
www.senseiselfdevelopment.care

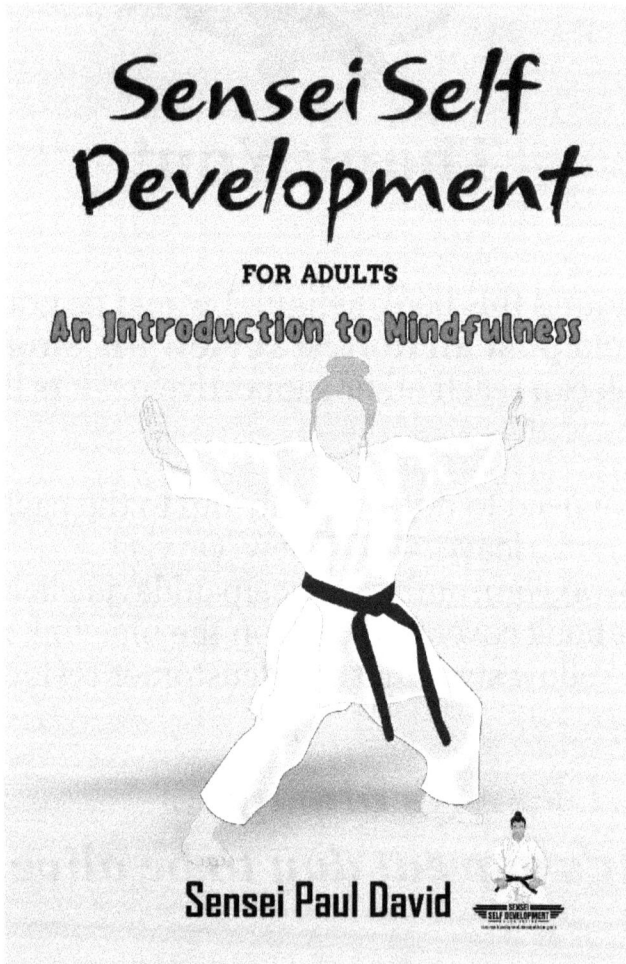

Sensei Self Development

FOR ADULTS

An Introduction to Mindfulness

Sensei Paul David

Check Out The SSD Chronicles
Series CLICK HERE

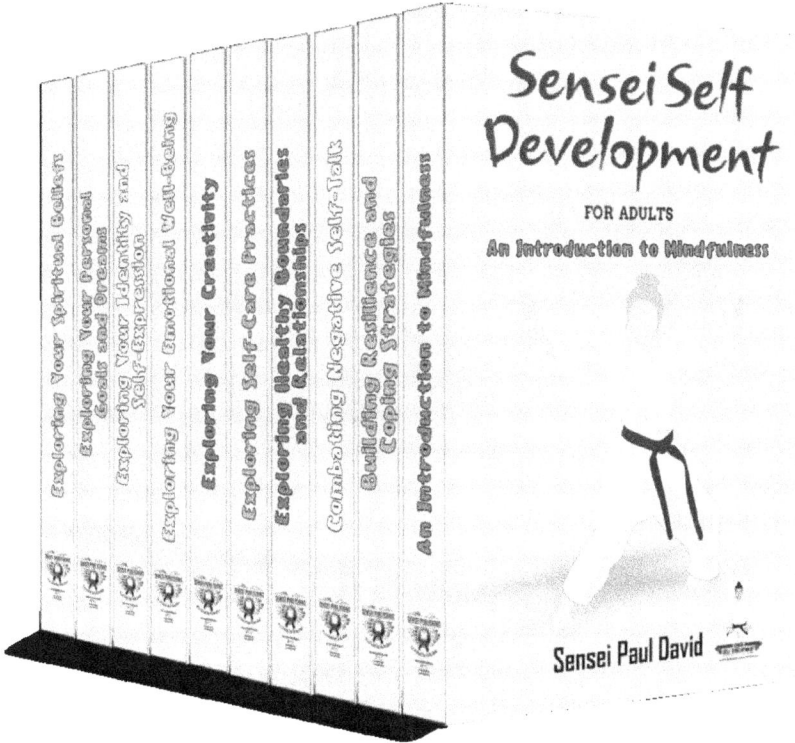

Exploring Your Spiritual Beliefs

Exploring Your Personal Goals and Dreams

Exploring Your Identity and Self-Expression

Exploring Your Emotional Well-Being

Exploring Your Creativity

Exploring Self-Care Practices

Exploring Healthy Boundaries and Relationships

Combating Negative Self-Talk

Building Resilience and Coping Strategies

An Introduction to Mindfulness

Sensei Self Development

FOR ADULTS

An Introduction to Mindfulness

Sensei Paul David

Get/Share Your FREE All-Ages Mental Health eBook Now at

www.senseiselfdevelopment.com

Or CLICK HERE

senseiselfdevelopment.com

Click Another Book In The SSD BOOK SERIES:

senseipublishing.com/SSD_SERIES

CLICK HERE

SENSEI SELF DEVELOPMENT

BOOKS SERIES

senseiselfdevelopment.senseipublishing.com

Join Our Publishing Journey!

If you would like to receive FREE BOOKS, please visit **www.senseipublishing.com**. Join our newsletter by entering your email address in the pop-up box

Follow Sensei Paul David on Amazon

CLICK THE LOGO BELOW

FREE BONUS!!!
Experience Over 25 FREE Engaging Guided Meditations!

Prized Skills & Practices for Adults & Kids. Help Restore Deep-Sleep, Lower Stress, Improve Posture, Navigate Uncertainty & More.

Download the Free Insight Timer App and click the link below:
http://insig.ht/sensei_paul

About Sensei Publishing

Sensei Publishing commits itself to helping people of all ages transform into better versions of themselves by providing high-quality and research-based self-development books with an emphasis on mental health and guided meditations. Sensei Publishing offers well-written e-books, audiobooks, paperbacks and online courses that simplify complicated but practical topics in line with its mission to inspire people towards positive transformation.

It's a great day to be alive!

About the Author

I create simple & transformative eBooks & Guided Meditations for Adults & Children proven to help navigate uncertainty, solve niche problems & bring families closer together.

I'm a former finance project manager, private pilot, jiu-jitsu instructor, musician & former University of Toronto Fitness Trainer. I prefer a science-based approach to focus on these & other areas in my life to stay humble & hungry to evolve. I hope you enjoy my work and I'd love to hear your feedback.

- It's a great day to be alive!

Sensei Paul David

Scan & Follow/Like/Subscribe: Facebook, Instagram, YouTube: @senseipublishing

Scan using your phone/iPad camera for Social Media
Visit us at www.senseipublishing.com and sign up for our
newsletter to learn more about our exciting books and to
experience our FREE Guided Meditations for Kids & Adults.

www.ingramcontent.com/pod-product-compliance
Lightning Source LLC
Chambersburg PA
CBHW071244020426
42333CB00015B/1615